KIDS ON EARTH

Wildlife Adventures – Explore The World
Puffin - Iceland

Sensei Paul David

COPYRIGHT PAGE

Kids On Earth: Wildlife Adventures - Explore The World

Puffin - Iceland

by Sensei Paul David,

Copyright © 2023.

All rights reserved.

978-1-77848-167-3 KoE_WildLife_Amazon_PaperbackBook_iceland_puffin

978-1-77848-166-6 KoE_WildLife_Amazon_eBook_iceland_puffin

978-1-77848-415-5 KoE_Wildlife_Ingram_Paperbackbook_IcelandPuffinBird

This book is not authorized for free distribution copying.

www.senseipublishing.com

@senseipublishing
#senseipublishing

Synopsis

This book is an introduction to the puffin in Iceland, a beloved seabird that lives off the coast of the island nation. It contains 30 unique and fun facts about the puffin, including its black and white pattern, its ability to dive up to 200 feet deep in search of food, its social behavior, and its importance to the Icelandic economy. The book also includes an introduction and conclusion that explain why the puffin is so special and why it is worth learning about.

Get Our FREE Books Now!

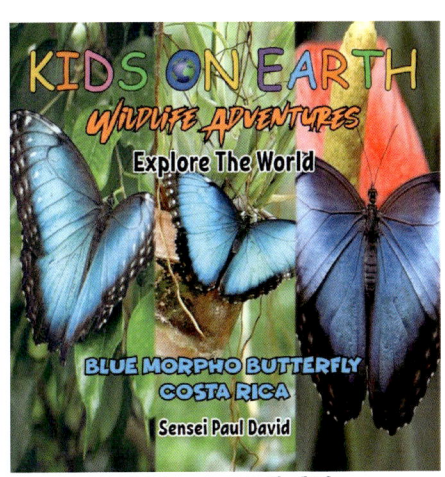

kidsonearth.life

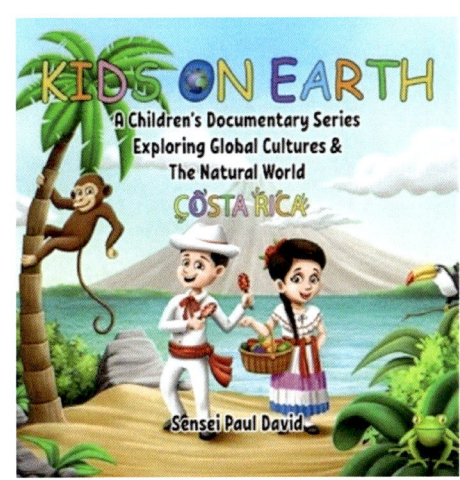

kidsonearth.world

Click Below for Another Book In Each Series

senseipublishing.com/KoE_SERIES

senseipublishing.com/KoE_Wildlife_SERIES

KoE En Español

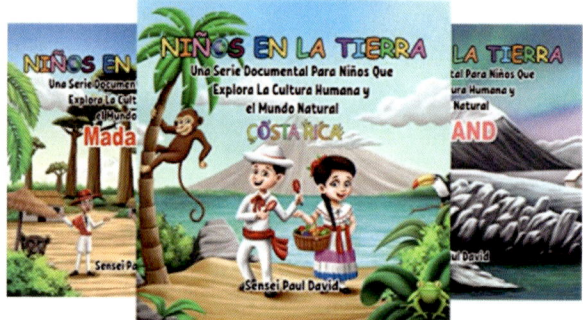

senseipublishing.com/KoE_SERIES_SPANISH

www.senseipublishing.com

Join Our Publishing Journey!

If you would like to receive FUTURE FREE BOOKS and get to know us better, please click www.senseipublishing.com and join our newsletter by entering your email address in the pop-up box.

Follow Our Blog: senseipauldavid.ca

Follow/Like/Subscribe: Facebook, Instagram, YouTube: @senseipublishing

Scan the QR Code with your phone or tablet to follow us on social media:

Like / Subscribe / Follow

Introduction

Hello! Welcome to the world of puffins! This book is about a very special bird that lives off the coast of Iceland. It is a small, chubby seabird that is beloved by people all over the world. Puffins are known for their playful personalities and bright, colorful feathers. Did you know that the puffin population in Iceland is growing? In this book, you will learn 30 unique and fun facts about the puffin in Iceland!

Puffins have a unique black and white pattern that helps them blend in with their rocky habitat.

Puffins are excellent swimmers and can dive up to 200 feet deep in search of food!

Puffins eat a variety of fish, including herring, capelin, and sand eel.

Puffins mate for life and build their nest on cliff ledges.

Puffins can live up to 25 years in the wild!

Puffins have a very special beak that is bright orange during the breeding season.

Puffins use their beaks to catch and carry their food back to their nest.

Puffins are very social birds and live in large colonies.

Puffins migrate south during the winter months.

Puffins are very noisy birds and can often be heard making loud calls.

Puffins can fly up to 30 miles per hour.

Puffins have a special form of communication called "billing" which they use to greet each other.

Puffins breed between May and August.

Puffins lay one egg per year and the chicks hatch after about six weeks.

Puffins are a keystone species, meaning their presence helps to maintain the balance of the marine ecosystem.

Puffins use their webbed feet to "fly" underwater in search of food.

Puffins are expert fishers and can catch more than one fish at a time.

Puffins are monogamous, meaning they mate for life.

Puffins spend most of their time at sea, but return to land to breed.

Puffins use their bright beaks to attract a mate.

Puffins can recognize their own chicks by their calls.

Puffins can live up to 60 years with the right care.

Puffins prefer to nest in isolated colonies away from predators.

Puffins have a special oil gland that helps them waterproof their feathers.

Puffins have a thick layer of down feathers to keep them warm in cold waters.

Puffins can fly as far as 1,200 miles in a single day.

Puffins use their wings to "row" underwater in search of food.

Puffins use their beaks to defend themselves from predators.

Puffins are a protected species in Iceland and are monitored by the government.

Puffins play a vital role in the Icelandic economy, as their feathers are used for traditional clothing and crafts.

Conclusion

We hope you enjoyed learning about the puffin in Iceland. They are a unique and fascinating bird that is beloved by people all over the world. Now that you know more about them, maybe you'll be inspired to visit Iceland and see them in their natural habitat!

Thank you for reading this book!

If you found this book helpful, I would be grateful if you would **post an honest review on Amazon** so this book can reach other supportive readers like you!

All you need to do is digitally flip to the back and leave your review. Or visit amazon.com/author/senseipauldavid click the correct book cover and click on the blue link next to the yellow stars that say, "customer reviews."

As always...

It's a great day to be alive!

Share Our FREE eBooks Now!

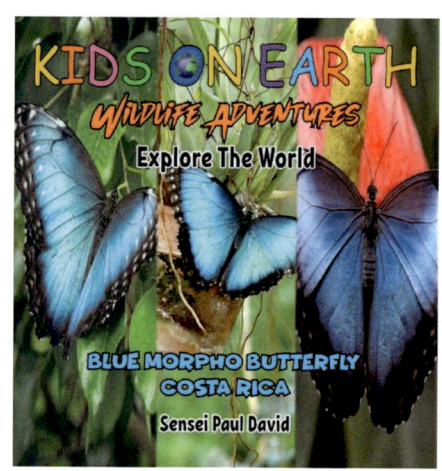

kidsonearth.life

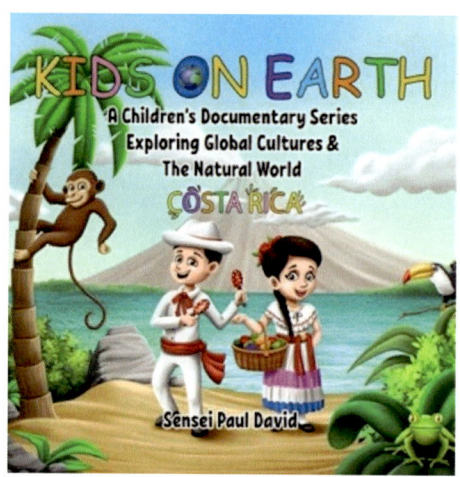

kidsonearth.world

Click Below for Another Book In Each Series

senseipublishing.com/KoE_SERIES

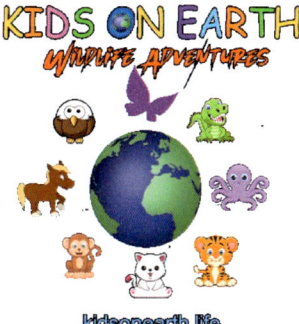

senseipublishing.com/KoE_Wildlife_SERIES

KoE En Español

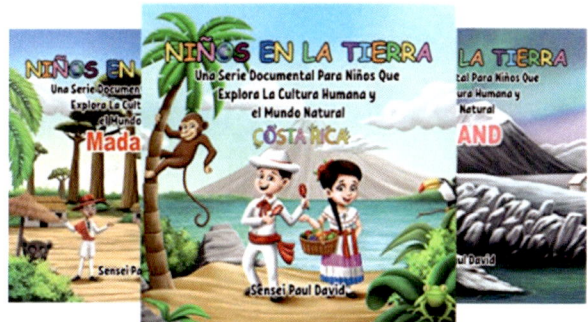

senseipublishing.com/KoE_SERIES_SPANISH

www.senseipublishing.com

www.senseipublishing.com

@senseipublishing
#senseipublishing

Check out our **recommendations** for other books for adults & kids plus other great resources by visiting
www.senseipublishing.com/resources/

Join Our Publishing Journey!

If you would like to receive FREE BOOKS and special offers, please visit www.senseipublishing.com and join our newsletter by entering your email address in the pop-up box

Follow Our Engaging Blog NOW!
senseipauldavid.ca

Get Our FREE Books Today!

Click & Share the Links Below

FREE Kids Books
lifeofbailey.senseipublishing.com
kidsonearth.senseipublishing.com

FREE Self-Development Book

senseiselfdevelopment.senseipublishing.com

FREE BONUS!!!
Experience Over 25 FREE Engaging Guided Meditations!

Prized Skills & Practices for Adults & Kids. Help Restore Deep Sleep, Lower Stress, Improve Posture, Navigate Uncertainty & More.

Download the Free Insight Timer App and click the link below:
http://insig.ht/sensei_paul

About Sensei Publishing

Sensei Publishing commits itself to helping people of all ages transform into better versions of themselves by providing high-quality and research-based self-development books with an emphasis on mental health and guided meditations. Sensei Publishing offers well-written e-books, audiobooks, paperbacks, and online courses that simplify complicated but practical topics in line with its mission to inspire people toward positive transformation.

It's a great day to be alive!

About the Author

I create simple & transformative eBooks & Guided Meditations for Adults & Children proven to help navigate uncertainty, solve niche problems & bring families closer together.

I'm a former finance project manager, private pilot, jiu-jitsu instructor, musician & former University of Toronto Fitness Trainer. I prefer a science-based approach to focus on these & other areas in my life to stay humble & hungry to evolve. I hope you enjoy my work and I'd love to hear your feedback.

- It's a great day to be alive!
Sensei Paul David

Scan & Follow/Like/Subscribe: Facebook, Instagram, YouTube: @senseipublishing

Scan using your phone/iPad camera for Social Media
Visit us at www.senseipublishing.com and sign up for our newsletter to learn more about our exciting books and to experience our FREE Guided Meditations for Kids & Adults.

www.ingramcontent.com/pod-product-compliance
Lightning Source LLC
Chambersburg PA
CBRC090902080526
44587CB00008B/166